Reading Street

Program Authors

Peter Afflerbach

Camille Blachowicz

Candy Dawson Boyd

Elena Izquierdo

Connie Juel

Edward Kame'enui

Donald Leu

Jeanne R. Paratore

P. David Pearson

Sam Sebesta

Deborah Simmons

Alfred Tatum

Sharon Vaughn

Susan Watts Taffe

Karen Kring Wixson

D1530912

PEARSON

Glenview, Illinois • Boston, Massachusetts • Chandler, Arizona • Upper Saddle River, New Jersey

We dedicate Reading Street to
Peter Jovanovich.

His wisdom, courage,
and passion for education
are an inspiration to us all.

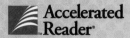

About the Cover Artist
Rob Hefferan likes to reminisce about the simple life he had as a child growing up in Cheshire, when his biggest worry was whether to have fish fingers or Alphabetti Spaghetti for tea. The faces, colors, and shapes from that time are a present-day inspiration for his artwork.

ISBN-13: 978-0-328-47852-1
ISBN-10:   0-328-47852-0
3 4 5 6 7 8 9 10 V042 14 13 12 11 10
CC1

Reading STREET

Dear Texas Reader,

All aboard, readers! We will be thinking and talking about how to get from here to there. We will be taking a train, riding in trucks, and making a rescue at sea.

Do you have all of your letters, words, and sentences ready to use? Remember, AlphaBuddy and your *My Skills Buddy* will be there to help you.

Away we go!

Sincerely,
The Authors

Going Places

 How do people and things get from here to there?

Week 2

Trade Book

Nonfiction • Social Studies
Mayday! Mayday! by Chris L. Demarest

Unit 5 Contents

Week 5

Week 6

Don Leu
The Internet Guy

Right before our eyes, the nature of reading and learning is changing. The Internet and other technologies create new opportunities, new solutions, and new literacies. New reading comprehension skills are required online. They are increasingly important to our students and our society.

Those of us on the Reading Street team are here to help you on this new, and very exciting, journey.

See It!

- Big Question Video

- Concept Talk Video

- Envision It! Animations

- eReaders

Hear It!

- *Sing with Me* Animations

- eSelections

- Grammar Jammer

Adam and Kim **play at the beach.**

Concept Talk Video

File   Edit   View   Favorites   Tools   Help

http://www.TexasReadingStreet.com

Do It!

- **Story Sort**

- **eReaders**

- **Letter Tile Drag and Drop**   o s c m s

Going Places

THE BIG

How do people and things get from here to there?

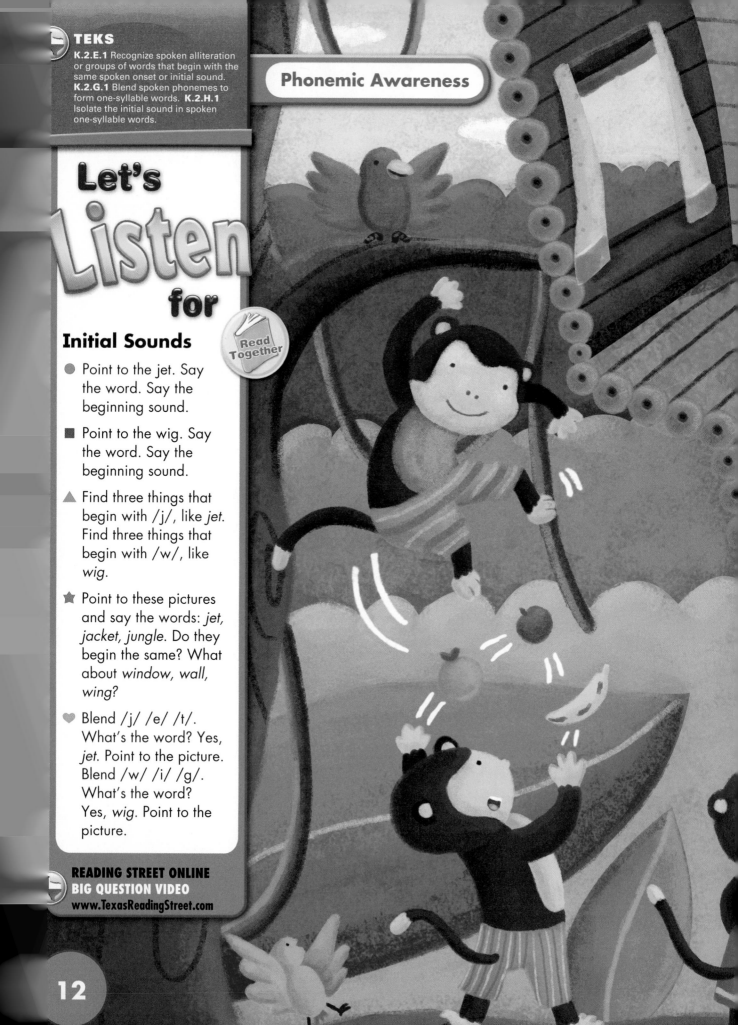

TEKS
K.2.E.1 Recognize spoken alliteration or groups of words that begin with the same spoken onset or initial sound. **K.2.G.1** Blend spoken phonemes to form one-syllable words. **K.2.H.1** Isolate the initial sound in spoken one-syllable words.

Phonemic Awareness

Let's Listen for

Initial Sounds

Read Together

- Point to the jet. Say the word. Say the beginning sound.

- Point to the wig. Say the word. Say the beginning sound.

- Find three things that begin with /j/, like *jet*. Find three things that begin with /w/, like *wig*.

- Point to these pictures and say the words: *jet, jacket, jungle*. Do they begin the same? What about *window, wall, wing*?

- Blend /j/ /e/ /t/. What's the word? Yes, *jet*. Point to the picture. Blend /w/ /i/ /g/. What's the word? Yes, *wig*. Point to the picture.

READING STREET ONLINE
BIG QUESTION VIDEO
www.TexasReadingStreet.com

TEKS

★ Determine whether a story is real or make-believe and tell why.

Comprehension

Envision It!

Realism and Fantasy

READING STREET ONLINE
ENVISION IT! ANIMATIONS
www.TexasReadingStreet.com

TEKS

K.3.A.1 Identify the common sounds that letters represent. **K.3.B.1** Use knowledge of letter-sound relationships to decode regular words in text and independent of content.

Envision It! | Sounds to Know

Ww

watermelon

Jj

jaguar

**READING STREET ONLINE
ALPHABET CARDS**
www.TexasReadingStreet.com

Phonics

Initial *Ww*, Initial *Jj*

Words I Can Blend

w   i   n

w   e   l   l

w   e   t

j   e   t

J   e   n

Words I Can Read

yellow

blue

green

Sentences I Can Read

1. They see a blue jet.

2. The sun is yellow.

3. I like the green jet.

TEKS
K.3.A.1 Identify the common sounds that letters represent. **K.3.B.1** Use knowledge of letter-sound relationships to decode regular words in text. **K.3.D** Identify and read at least 25 high-frequency words from a commonly used list.

Phonics

I Can Read!

Decodable Reader

● Consonant *Ww*
Wes
wet
will

■ Consonant *Jj*
job
jet
Jen

▲ High-Frequency Words

a	the
yellow	with
blue	go
green	

★ Read the story.

**READING STREET ONLINE
DECODABLE eREADERS**
www.TexasReadingStreet.com

**Decodable
Reader
25**

On a Jet
Written by Mike O'Hern
Illustrated by Joan Tortle

Wes had a big job.
Wes got the yellow jet wet.

Wes will fill it.
Wes will fill it with gas.

Jen had a big job.
Jen sat in the blue jet.

Jen had a big grin.
Jen can hop in.
It can go fast.

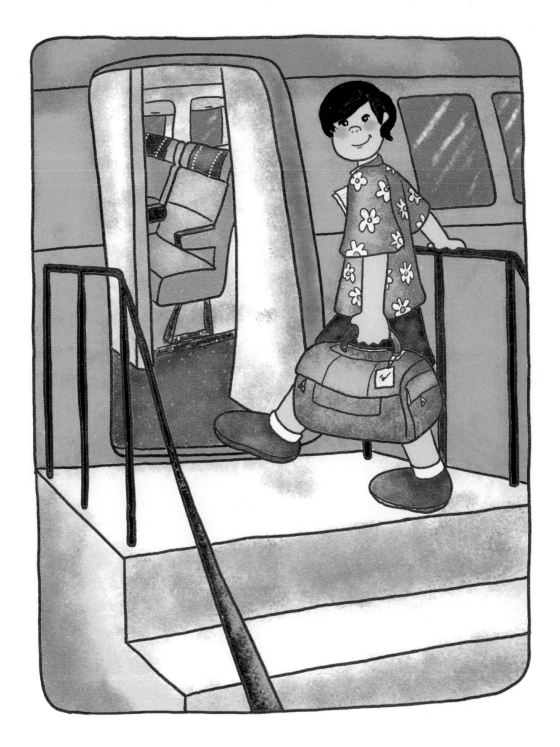

Wes had a big bag.
Wes got in the green jet.

Wes had a big grin.
It can go fast.

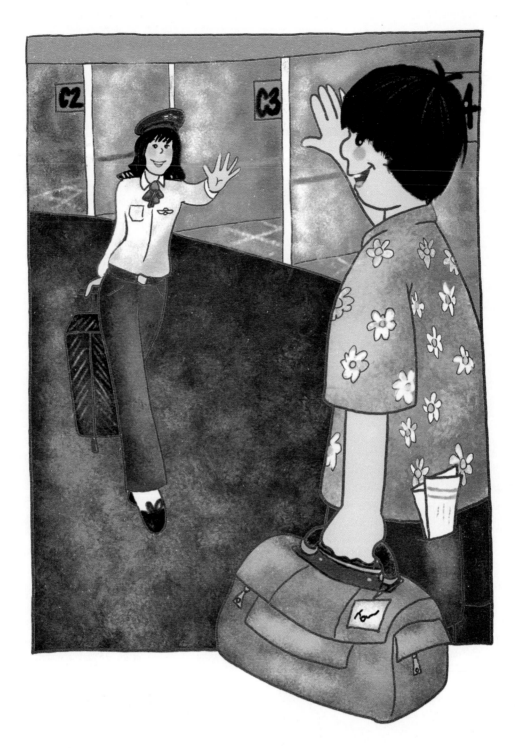

Wes met Jen.
Wes and Jen grin.

TEKS

K.8.A.1 Retell a main event from a story read aloud. **RC-K.E.1** Retell important events in stories. **RC-K.F.1** Make connections to own experiences. ★ Determine whether a story is real or make-believe and tell why.

Envision It! | Retell

Big Book

Think, Talk, and Write

1. Which are ways you have traveled? Text to Self

2. Which story is about real animals? Which is about make-believe animals?

Realism and Fantasy

3. Look back and write.

Let's Learn It!

Vocabulary

- Talk about the pictures.
- Which vehicles have you ridden in?

Listening and Speaking

- Who is a friend that lives close to you?
- What did you eat for breakfast?
- Where do we keep the art supplies in our classroom?
- When do we use an umbrella? Why do we use an umbrella?

Vocabulary

Transportation Words

airplane

truck

boat

train

Ask and Answer Questions

Be a good speaker!

TEKS
K.6.C.1 Recognize sensory details.
K.7.A Respond to rhythm and rhyme in poetry through identifying a regular beat and similarities in word sounds.

The Swing

Let's Practice It!

Poem

- ● Listen to the poem.
- ■ Swing your arms back and forth in time to its rhythm.
- ▲ Which word in the poem rhymes with *swing*? with *all*? with *brown*?
- ★ How do you know that the child is swinging very high in the air?

TEKS
K.2.C.1 Orally generate rhymes in response to spoken words.
K.2.G.1 Blend spoken phonemes to form one-syllable words.

Let's Listen for

Final Sounds

Read Together

- Point to a fox. Say *fox*. Say the last sound.

- Find three things that end with /ks/, like *fox*.

- Point to these things and say the words: *fix*, *ax*, *sax*. Do they end the same?

- Blend /f/ /o/ /ks/. What's the word? Yes, *fox*. Point to the picture.

- What rhymes with *fix*?

READING STREET ONLINE
BIG QUESTION VIDEO
www.TexasReadingStreet.com

32

33

TEKS
★ Identify what happens in a text and why it happens.

Comprehension

Envision It!

Cause and Effect

 READING STREET ONLINE
ENVISION IT! ANIMATIONS
www.TexasReadingStreet.com

35

TEKS

K.3.C.2 Recognize that new words are created when letters are added.
K.3.D.1 Identify and read at least 25 high-frequency words from a commonly used list. **Also K.3.B.1.**

Envision It! | Sounds to Know

Xx

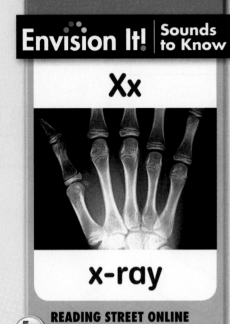

x-ray

READING STREET ONLINE
ALPHABET CARDS
www.TexasReadingStreet.com

Phonics

Final Xx

Words I Can Blend

s   i   x

o   x

f   o   x

b   o   x

w   a   x

Words I Can Read

yellow

blue

green

Sentences I Can Read

1. That box is yellow.

2. The green box is big.

3. Fox is in the blue box.

TEKS

K.3.A.1 Identify the common sounds that letters represent. **K.3.B.1** Use knowledge of letter-sound relationships to decode regular words in text. **K.3.D** Identify and read at least 25 high-frequency words from a commonly used list.

Phonics

Decodable Reader

- Consonant *Xx*
  Fox
  fix
  box
  Ox

- High-Frequency Words

a	blue
yellow	to
green	have
is	the

▲ Read the story.

Decodable Reader 26

Fox Can Fix It!

Written by Roger Bines
Illustrated by Chris Lemon

Pig had a blue and yellow cap.
It had a rip in it.
Get it to Fox. Fox can fix it.

Did Fox fix it?
Fox did!

Cat had a green box.
It did not have a top.
Get it to Fox. Fox can fix it.

Did Fox fix it?
Fox did!

Ox is hot.
The fan is not on.
Get it to Fox. Fox can fix it.

Did Fox fix it?
Fox did.

Fox sat.
Fox can fix it!

TEKS

K.10.B.1 Retell important facts in a text, heard or read. **RC-K.F.3** Make connections to the larger community. **RC-K.F.4** Discuss textual evidence. ★ Identify what happens in a text and why it happens.

Envision It! | Retell

Trade Book

READING STREET ONLINE
STORY SORT
www.TexasReadingStreet.com

Think, Talk, and Write

1. How can a helicopter help in an emergency? **Text to World**

2. In *Mayday! Mayday!* the Coast Guard rescues sailors. What happened that made the sailors need help?

🔄 **Cause and Effect**

3. Look back and write.

TEKS

K.5.A Identify and use words that name positions. **K.23** Follow agreed-upon rules for discussion, including taking turns and speaking one at a time.

Let's Learn It!

Vocabulary

- Talk about the pictures.
- ■ Point to the top book in the stack.
- ▲ Point to the bottom book in the stack.
- ★ Touch the front of a book.
- ♥ Touch the back of a book.

Listening and Speaking

- What happens in the story?
- ■ Who are the people in the story?
- ▲ Pretend you are the people in the story. Act out what happens.

Vocabulary

Position Words

top

bottom

front

back

Respond to Literature
Drama

Be a good listener!

TEKS

K.6.A Identify elements of a story including character and key events. **K.6.B** Discuss the big idea of a well-known fable and connect it to personal experience. **K.8.B.1** Describe characters in a story. **RC-K.E.2** Act out important events in stories.

The Wind and the Sun

Let's
Practice
It!

1

Fable

- Listen to the fable.

- Who are the main characters? How are they different from characters in other stories you have read?

- With two friends, act out the fable.

- What lesson does the fable teach?

51

TEKS

K.2.E.1 Recognize spoken alliteration or groups of words that begin with the same spoken onset or initial sound. **K.2.G.1** Blend spoken phonemes to form one-syllable words. **K.2.H.1** Isolate the initial sound in spoken one-syllable words.

Let's Listen for

Initial Sounds

Read Together

● Point to the man going up the ladder. Say *up*. Say the beginning sound.

■ Find three things that begin with /u/, like *up*.

▲ Point to these pictures and say the words: *up, shoe, underground.* Do they begin the same? What about *unhappy, umbrella, under*?

★ Blend /u/ /p/. What's the word? Yes, *up*.

READING STREET ONLINE
BIG QUESTION VIDEO
www.TexasReadingStreet.com

52

TEKS

★ Tell how facts, ideas, characters, settings, or events are the same and/or different.

Comprehension

Envision It!

Compare and Contrast

 READING STREET ONLINE
ENVISION IT! ANIMATIONS
www.TexasReadingStreet.com

54

TEKS

K.3.A.1 Identify the common sounds that letters represent.
K.3.B.1 Use letter-sound relationships to decode regular words in text.
K.3.C.3 Recognize that new words are created when letters are deleted.

Envision It! | **Sounds to Know**

Uu

umbrella

READING STREET ONLINE
ALPHABET CARDS
www.TexasReadingStreet.com

Phonics

Short *u*

Words I Can Blend

Words I Can Read

what

said

was

Sentences I Can Read

1. What can the pup do?

2. Gus said, "Pups run."

3. The pup was fun.

TEKS

K.3.A.1 Identify the common sounds that letters represent. **K.3.B.1** Use knowledge of letter-sound relationships to decode regular words in text. **K.3.D** Identify and read at least 25 high-frequency words from a commonly used list.

Phonics

I Can Read!

Decodable Reader

● Short *Uu*

Bud	pup	up
ruff	run	jump
sun	dug	mud
fun	tub	hug

■ High-Frequency Words

is	a
said	what
see	the
was	

▲ Read the story.

Fun for Bud

Written by Judy Wienhouse
Illustrated by Gabrial Peterson

Decodable Reader 27

Bud is a pup.
Bud sat up.
Bud said, "Ruff, ruff."

What did Bud see?
Run, Bud, run.

Bud can run fast.
Bud can jump up.

Bud sat in the sun.
It was hot.
Bud got wet.

Bud dug in mud.
Bud had fun.

Get Bud in the tub.
Get Bud wet.

Bud can get a big hug.
Bud can get in bed.

TEKS
K.10.B.1 Retell important facts from a text, heard or read.
RC-K.F.3 Make connections to the larger community. ★ Tell how facts, ideas, characters, settings, or events are the same and/or different.

Envision It! | Retell

Big Book

1

2

3

4

5

6

 READING STREET ONLINE
STORY SORT
www.TexasReadingStreet.com

66

Think, Talk, and Write

1. How do trucks help people do their jobs? Text to World

2. How are these trucks from *Trucks Roll!* alike? How are they different?

Compare and Contrast

3. Look back and write.

TEKS

K.23 Follow agreed-upon rules for discussion, including taking turns and speaking one at a time.

Let's Learn It!

Vocabulary

- Talk about the pictures.
- Which job would you like to do?

Listening and Speaking

- How does a truck move?
- Act out how a truck driver does his or her job.

Words for Jobs

pilot

truck driver

conductor

astronaut

Discuss Literature

Be a good listener!

TEKS

K.9.A.1 Identify the topic of an informational text heard. **K.11.B.2** Identify the meaning of specific signs. **RC-K.A** Discuss purposes for reading and listening to various texts.

Going Downtown

LIBRARY

Let's Practice It!

Signs

● Listen to the selection.

■ What is the selection about?

▲ Point to each sign. Tell what it means.

★ What do you notice about signs 1 and 5? about signs 2 and 4?

♥ Why are signs like these important?

ONE WAY

BANK

P

PARKING GARAGE

71

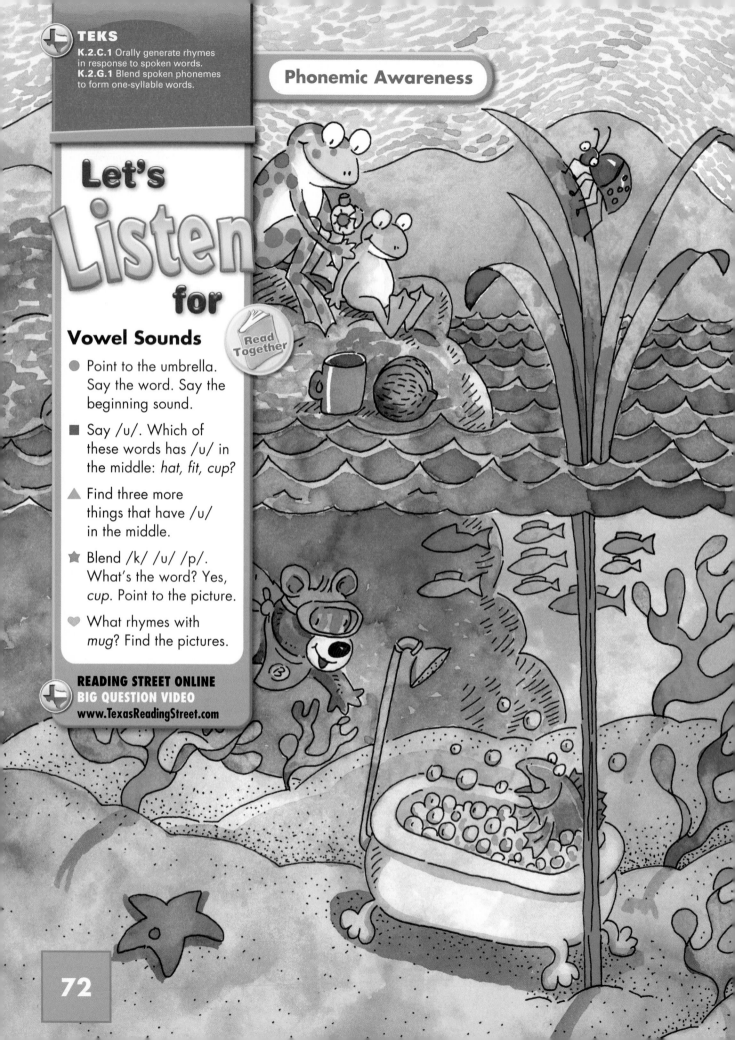

TEKS
K.2.C.1 Orally generate rhymes in response to spoken words.
K.2.G.1 Blend spoken phonemes to form one-syllable words.

Phonemic Awareness

Let's Listen for

Read Together

Vowel Sounds

● Point to the umbrella. Say the word. Say the beginning sound.

■ Say /u/. Which of these words has /u/ in the middle: *hat, fit, cup?*

▲ Find three more things that have /u/ in the middle.

★ Blend /k/ /u/ /p/. What's the word? Yes, *cup.* Point to the picture.

♥ What rhymes with *mug?* Find the pictures.

READING STREET ONLINE
BIG QUESTION VIDEO
www.TexasReadingStreet.com

TEKS
K.6.A.3 Identify elements of a story including key events.

Comprehension

Envision It!

Literary Elements

READING STREET ONLINE
ENVISION IT! ANIMATIONS
www.TexasReadingStreet.com

Characters

Setting

Plot

TEKS

K.3.C.1 Recognize that new words are created when letters are changed.
K.3.D.1 Identify and read at least 25 high-frequency words from a commonly used list.

Envision It! | Sounds to Know

Uu

umbrella

**READING STREET ONLINE
ALPHABET CARDS**
www.TexasReadingStreet.com

Phonics

Short *u*

Words I Can Blend

m u g

b u g

r u g

d u g

m u d

Words I Can Read

what

said

was

Sentences I Can Read

1. What is in the tub?

2. "It is a pet," said Bud.

3. Was the pet in mud?

TEKS

K.3.A.1 Identify the common sounds that letters represent. **K.3.B.1** Use knowledge of letter-sound relationships to decode regular words in text. **K.3.D** Identify and read at least 25 high-frequency words from a commonly used list.

Phonics

I Can Read!

Decodable Reader

● Short *Uu*

bus	sub	drum
bug	fun	cup
mud	tub	

■ High-Frequency Words

the	what
do	I
said	have
was	a

▲ Read the story.

Jan at the Fair

Written by Josh Dart
Illustrated by Dave Goodman

Decodable Reader 28

Jan sat on the bus.
What will Jan do?

"Can I get in the sub?" said Jan.
Jan will get in.

Jan can hit the drum.
Jan will grin.

Jan can hop on the bug.
Jan will have fun.

Jan can sip.
The red cup was big.

Jan can drop mud in a tub.
Jan will get it in.

Jan can get on the bus.
Jan had fun!

TEKS

K.6.A.3 Identify elements of a story including key events. **K.8.A.1** Retell a main event from a story read aloud. **RC-K.E.2** Act out important events in stories. **RC-K.F.2** Make connections to ideas in other texts.

Envision It! | Retell

Trade Book

READING STREET ONLINE
STORY SORT
www.TexasReadingStreet.com

86

Think, Talk, and Write

1. Does *The Little Engine That Could* remind you of another story we have read? Which one? **Text to Text**

2.
Beginning	
Middle	
End	

Choose an important part of the story. Act it out with some friends. ↺ **Plot**

3. Look back and write.

Let's Learn It!

Vocabulary
- Talk about the picture.
- On which days of the week do we come to school?
- On which days do we stay home?

Listening and Speaking
- What happens first in the story?
- What happens next in the story?
- Then what happens in the story?
- What happens last in the story?

Vocabulary

Time Words

April

Sunday	Monday	Tuesday	Wednesday	Thursday	Friday	Saturday
					1	2
3	4	5	6	7	8	9
10	11	12	13	14	15	16

Sequence

Be a good
listener!

TEKS

K.6.D Recognize recurring phrases and characters in traditional folk tales from various cultures. **K.8.B.1** Describe the characters in a story.

Queen of the Forest

Let's Practice It!

Folk Tale

● Listen to the folk tale.

■ Which words give you a clue that this is a folk tale?

▲ How would you describe Tiger? How would you describe Fox?

★ How are this folk tale and "How the Fly Saved the River" alike?

①

TEKS

K.2.E.1 Recognize spoken alliteration or groups of words that begin with the same spoken onset or initial sound.
K.2.H.1 Isolate the initial sound in spoken one-syllable words.

Phonemic Awareness

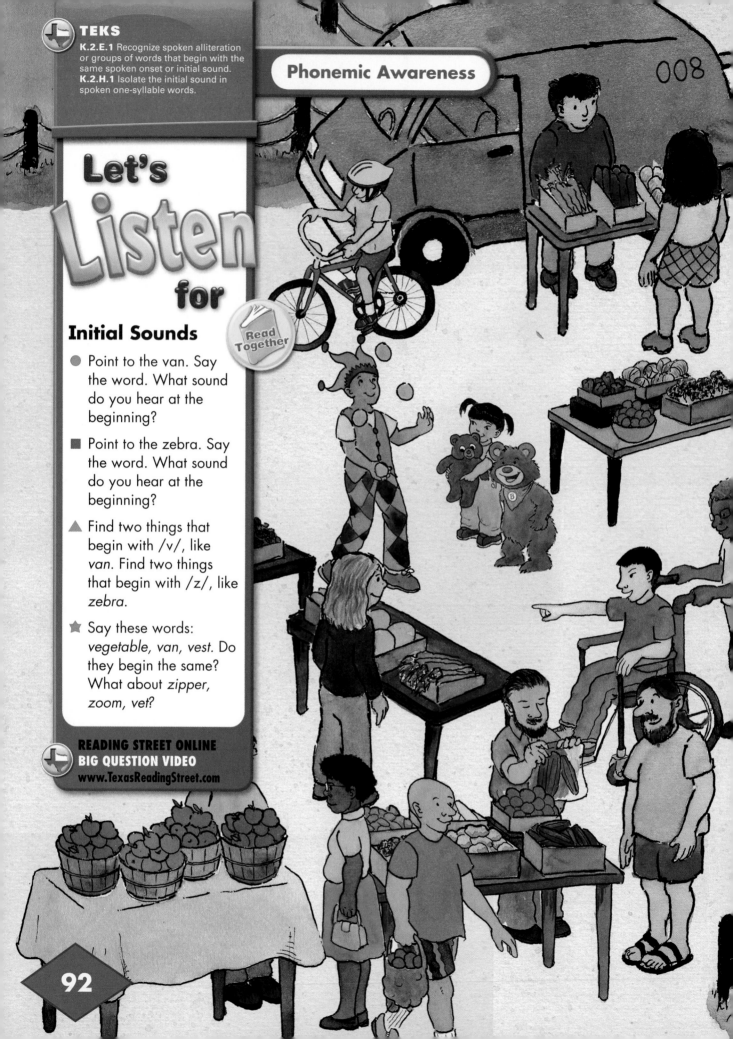

Let's Listen for

Read Together

Initial Sounds

● Point to the van. Say the word. What sound do you hear at the beginning?

■ Point to the zebra. Say the word. What sound do you hear at the beginning?

▲ Find two things that begin with /v/, like *van*. Find two things that begin with /z/, like *zebra*.

★ Say these words: *vegetable, van, vest.* Do they begin the same? What about *zipper, zoom, vet?*

READING STREET ONLINE
BIG QUESTION VIDEO
www.TexasReadingStreet.com

Comprehension

Envision It!

Main Idea

READING STREET ONLINE
ENVISION IT! ANIMATIONS
www.TexasReadingStreet.com

School

TEKS

K.3.B.1 Use letter-sound relationships to decode regular words in text.
K.3.C.1 Recognize that new words are created when letters are changed.
K.3.D.1 Identify and read at least 25 high-frequency words from a commonly used list.

Envision It! | Sounds to Know

Vv

volcano

READING STREET ONLINE
ALPHABET CARDS
www.TexasReadingStreet.com

Phonics

Initial Vv, Initial Zz

Words I Can Blend

Words I Can Read

where

come

Sentences I Can Read

1. Where is Zak?

2. He will come in a van.

3. Val can not come.

TEKS

K.3.A.1 Identify the common sounds that letters represent. K.3.B.1 Use knowledge of letter-sound relationships to decode regular words in text. K.3.D Identify and read at least 25 high-frequency words from a commonly used list.

Phonics

I Can Read!

Decodable Reader

- ● Consonant *Vv*

  Val

- ■ Consonant *Zz*

  zip

- ▲ High-Frequency Words

is	where
a	here
with	come
do	

- ★ Read the story.

- ♥ After reading, retell the story.

Zip Up, Val!

Written by Susan Whit
Illustrated by Kevin Kessler

Decodable Reader 29

Zip up, Val.
It is not hot.
Val ran.

Val got in it.
Zip up, Val.
It is not hot.

Zip up, Val.
It is not hot.
Val ran.

Val got in it.
Zip up, Val.
It is not hot.

Where is it hot?
Dad had a map.
It can get hot here.

Val got on a jet.
Val got on a jet with Dad.

Come here, Val.
Do not zip up, Val.
It is hot!

TEKS

K.10.A Identify the topic and details in expository text heard or read, referring to the words and/or illustrations. **K.10.B.1** Retell important facts in a text, heard or read. **RC-K.F.3** Make connections to the larger community.

Big Book

Envision It! | Retell

1

2

3

4

5

6

Think, Talk, and Write

1. When might someone take a plane to travel? When would they take a bus?

Text to World

2. What is the selection *On the Move!* mostly about?

 Main Idea

3. Look back and write.

107

TEKS

K.5.B Recognize that compound words are made up of shorter words. **K.21.A.1** Listen attentively by facing speakers. **K.22** Share information and ideas by speaking audibly and clearly using the conventions of language.

Let's Learn It!

Vocabulary

- Talk about the pictures.
- Blend the words *dog* and *sled*.
- ▲ Segment the word *raincoat*.
- ★ Blend other compound words you know.

Listening and Speaking

- Tell three things about someone or something in the story.
- Tell about your favorite food.

Vocabulary

Compound Words

dog **+** sled **=**

dogsled

rain **+** coat **=**

raincoat

mail **+** box **=** mailbox

Oral Presentation
Description

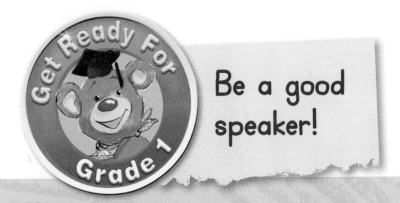

Be a good speaker!

TEKS

K.2.C.1 Orally generate rhymes in response to spoken words.
K.6.D Recognize recurring phrases and characters in traditional lullabies from various cultures. **K.7.A.2** Respond to rhyme in poetry through identifying similarities in word sounds.

All the Pretty Little Horses

Let's Practice It!

Lullaby

● Listen to the lullaby.

■ What tells you this is a lullaby?

▲ Which words rhyme? Name another word that rhymes with each pair.

★ Why do we read, sing, or listen to lullabies?

Phonemic Awareness

Let's Listen for

Initial Sounds

Read Together

● Say the sound you hear at the beginning of *yard*. At the beginning of *question*.

■ Point to the yard. Find something else that begins like *yard*.

▲ Point to the question mark. Find something else that begins like *question*.

★ Name other words that begin with /y/ and with /kw/.

♥ Blend /y/ *-ell*. What's the word? Yes, *yell*. Blend /kw/ *-ick*. What's the word? Yes, *quick*.

READING STREET ONLINE
BIG QUESTION VIDEO
www.TexasReadingStreet.com

Comprehension

Envision It!

Draw Conclusions

**READING STREET ONLINE
ENVISION IT! ANIMATIONS**
www.TexasReadingStreet.com

Happy
Happy
Happy

TEKS

K.3.B.2 Use letter-sound relationships to decode regular words independent of content.
K.3.C.1 Recognize that new words are created when letters are changed.

Envision It! | **Sounds to Know**

Qq

queen

Yy

yo-yo

READING STREET ONLINE
ALPHABET CARDS
www.TexasReadingStreet.com

Phonics

Initial Qq, Initial Yy

Words I Can Blend

116

High-Frequency Words

Words I Can Read

where

come

Sentences I Can Read

1. Where is Quinn?
2. He did not come yet.
3. Will Quinn quit?

TEKS

K.3.A.1 Identify the common sounds that letters represent. **K.3.B.1** Use knowledge of letter-sound relationships to decode regular words in text. **K.3.D** Identify and read at least 25 high-frequency words from a commonly used list.

Phonics

I Can Read!

Decodable Reader

- Consonant *Yy*
  yes   yak

- Consonant *Qq*
  quiz   quit

- High-Frequency Words
  a
  come
  is
  said
  where
  the
  four

- Read the story.

READING STREET ONLINE
DECODABLE eREADERS
www.TexasReadingStreet.com

The Quiz

Written by Cathy Collins
Illustrated by Eric Mendez

Decodable Reader 30

Jim will get a quiz.
Jim and Mom come in.
Jim and Mom sit.

Can Mom help Jim?
Yes, Mom can help him.
Jim sat. Mom sat.

"Jim, is a yak an ox?"
Jim sat. Jim said,
"A yak is not an ox."

121

"Jim, where is the big yak?"
Jim sat. Jim said,
"The big yak is on top."

"Jim, add six plus four."
Jim sat.
Six plus four is ten.

Jim will quit.
Jim will run fast.
Jim will get on the bus.

Jim got the quiz.
Can Jim pass?
Yes, Jim did!

TEKS

K.10.B.1 Retell important facts in a text, heard or read. **RC-K.F.1** Make connections to own experiences.

Envision It! Retell

Trade Book

**READING STREET ONLINE
STORY SORT
www.TexasReadingStreet.com**

Think, Talk, and Write

1. How do you get to school?

Text to Self

2. Why do children in different parts of the world use different ways to get to school?

Draw Conclusions

3. Look back and write.

Let's Learn It!

Vocabulary

● Talk about the pictures.

■ When might you jump?

▲ When might you hop?

★ Let's try skipping around the room.

Listening and Speaking

● What happens first in the story?

■ What happens next in the story?

▲ Then what happens in the story?

★ What happens last in the story?

Vocabulary
Action Words

ride

jump

hop

climb

skip

Discuss Literary Features
Plot

Be a good listener!

TEKS
K.6.D Recognize recurring phrases and characters in traditional fairy tales from various cultures. **K.8.B** Describe characters in a story and the reasons for their actions.

The Dragon Test

Let's Practice It!

Fairy Tale

● Listen to the fairy tale.

■ How does the fairy tale begin and end?

▲ Which character would probably appear only in a fairy tale? Why?

★ Describe the eldest son and the middle son.

♥ Why does the king choose the youngest son?

1

2

3

Words for Things That Go

airplane

bike

truck

car

bus

van

boat

train

Words for Colors

white

purple

brown

green

black

pink

blue

red

yellow

orange

Words for Shapes

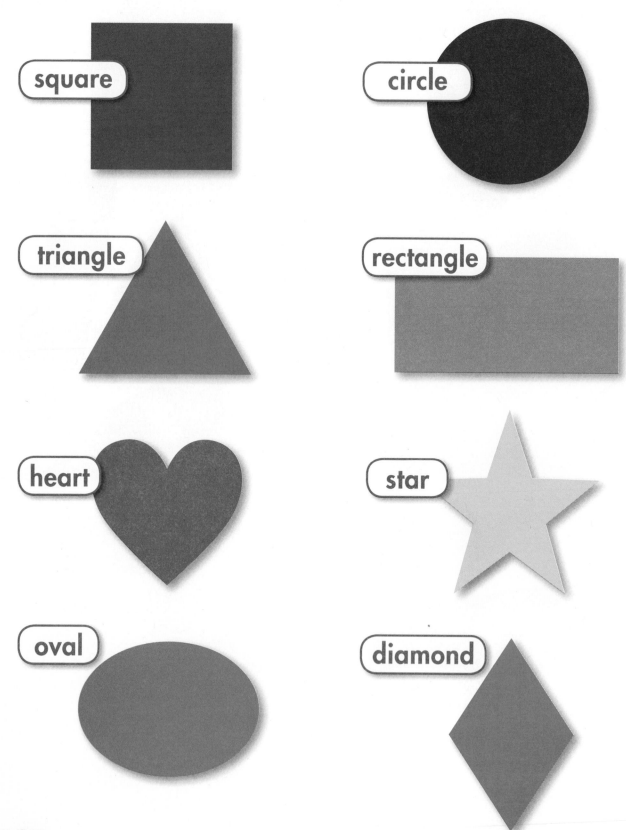

square

circle

triangle

rectangle

heart

star

oval

diamond

Words for Places

school

home

park

train station

police station

fire station

post office

library

Words for Animals

lion

mouse

puppy

dog

cat

kitten

duck

turtle

chick

hen

rooster

bird

butterfly

fish

whale

caterpillar

bear

panda

beaver

calf

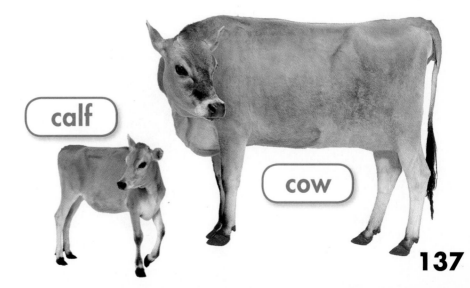

cow

Words for Actions

skip

walk

run

fly

swim

ride

jump

hop

Position Words

up

in

out

on

around

down

over

under

139

My Classroom

bookcase

easel

books

desk

markers

crayons

pencils

teacher

toys

paper

chair

blocks

table

rug

Words for Feelings

happy

frightened

worried

excited

angry

proud

sad

surprised

My Family

mom
mother

dad
father

sister

grandmother

grandfather

brother

Acknowledgments

Illustrations

Cover: Rob Hefferan

12, 59–65 Natalia Vasquez

19–25 Maria Mola

30 Julia Woolf

32 Paul Meisel

39–45 Cale Atkinson

50–51 Rob Hefferan

52 Mary Sullivan

70 Jan Bryan Hunt

72, 108 George Ulrich

79–85 Dani Jones

90–91 Ana Ochoa

92 Carol Koeller

99–105 Robbie Short

110 Leslie Harrington

112 Jamie Smith

119–125 Wednesday Kirwan

128 Anthony Lewis

130–131 Viviana Garofoli.

The *Texas Essential Knowledge and Skills for English Language Arts and Reading* reproduced by permission, Texas Education Agency, 1701 N. Congress Avenue, Austin, TX 78701

Photographs

Every effort has been made to secure permission and provide appropriate credit for photographic material. The publisher deeply regrets any omission and pledges to correct errors called to its attention in subsequent editions.

Unless otherwise acknowledged, all photographs are the property of Pearson Education, Inc.

Photo locators denoted as follows: Top (T), Center (C), Bottom (B), Left (L), Right (R), Background (Bkgd)

10 (B) ©Tim Bird/Corbis

28 ©Alex Segre/Alamy Images, ©moodboard/Corbis, ©Randy Faris/Corbis, ©Corbis/Jupiter Images

29 ©JG Photography/Alamy

48 Getty Images

68 ©Peter Titmuss/Alamy Images, ©Picture Contact/Alamy Images, Brand X Pictures, Jupiter Images.